Genre Fiction

Essential Question
What can we see in the sky?

A Different Set of Stars

by Loretta Wilcox

illustrated by Ann Iosa

"I'll miss you, Muffin." Anita hoped their neighbor would take good care of their cat while they were away.

The cat hopped off her lap and jumped into her open suitcase. "Isabel, look. The cat's coming with us," Anita joked.

But Anita's sister didn't smile. Isabel was checking her packing list again. She did not want to forget anything.

Anita and Isabel were twins. Isabel was three minutes older than Anita. She always seemed to enjoy bossing Anita around.

"Are you all packed?" Mom called from the hall.

"I am," said Isabel. She frowned at Anita. Anita looked at her suitcase. It was a mess.

The twins were going to Brazil
with their mother. She was a
photographer. She was going to take
pictures of birds that lived in the
Amazon jungle.

The girls were delighted. It was
going to be an adventure! The best
part was that they would be staying
two nights at a jungle lodge.

The flight was long, but the twins were too excited to feel sleepy. They finally arrived at the jungle lodge.

Mom got out her camera. The twins knew she was looking for birds to photograph.

They joined other guests sitting on the porch. They were all watching the sunset.

There was a tray of fruit smoothies on the table. A sign said: *Welcome Drinks*. Anita took one and had a big sip. "It's delicious," she said.

"I could get used to this," Isabel said, taking a drink for herself.

Anita finished her smoothie. Then she closed her eyes. She fell asleep and dreamed she was back home with Muffin.

Her mother's voice woke her. She opened her eyes. The other guests had gone.

"Let's go to our room," Mom said, taking Anita's hand. "We need to get dressed for dinner."

"Everything is so different here," Anita said after dinner. They were back on the porch. There were no electric lights, only moonlight and a few candles.

"That's not true," said Isabel. "The moon is the same." She liked correcting Anita.

But Anita did not enjoy being
corrected all the time. She looked
for the one star pattern she knew.
"I can't find the Big Dipper," Anita
grumbled. She turned to her sister.
"If you're so smart, why don't you
find it for us, Miss Know-it-all?"

"You won't find the Big Dipper here," said Mom. "We're south of the equator." She picked up an orange from the fruit bowl on the table. "Pretend this is Earth. Can you see why people here see a different set of stars?"

Anita looked at the orange. She imagined herself on the top half looking at the sky. Then she imagined herself on the bottom half. It made sense. People in this part of the world saw a different set of stars.

12

"So, the Big Dipper is still there,"
Anita reasoned. "But it's only visible
from the other half of the orange.
I mean Earth." She corrected herself
before her sister had the chance.

"Right!" said Mom. She pointed at a group of bright stars that formed the shape of a cross. "That's the Southern Cross."

"I've never seen that before,"
said Isabel.

"Well, you've never been on this side
of the orange before," said Anita. "I
mean *Earth*," she corrected herself.

Anita felt happy and a little bit
excited. She knew things were
different in different parts of the
world. But she had never thought
about a different set of stars.

Respond to Reading

Summarize

Use detailed information to summarize *A Different Set of Stars.*

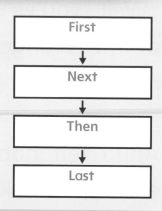

Text Evidence

1. How do you know *A Different Set of Stars* is fiction? Genre

2. What happens after Anita looks at the orange? Story details will help.
   Sequence

3. What is the meaning of the word *moonlight* on page 9? Compound Words

4. Write about what you think will happen next on the family's trip.
   Write About Reading

Compare Texts
Read more about stars.

Stars may look yellow, red, blue, or white.

Purestock/SuperStock

What Is a Star?

A star is a huge ball of hot gases. The hottest part is its center. Stars have a lot of energy, some of which is released as light. Starlight can be different colors.

17

Our Sun is a yellow star.

Our Sun

Do you think you can see stars only at nighttime? You might be forgetting one. We see one star every day. That star is the Sun. It looks bigger and brighter than other stars. But our Sun is not the biggest, brightest star in the sky. It's just much, much closer to us than any other star. It is the closest star to our planet.

Shooting stars are actually meteors.

What Is a Shooting Star?

A shooting star seems to be darting across the night sky. But shooting stars are not really stars. They are pieces of rock or dust. They hit Earth's atmosphere from space. Most burn up before they reach the ground. However, sometimes a part of a shooting star does reach Earth's surface.

Make Connections
What does Anita see in the sky?
Essential Question
Could Anita see a shooting star in Brazil? Text to Text

Focus on
Literary Elements

Plot The plot tells the story events in sequence: first, next, then, and last.

What to Look For Notice what the characters do, where they go, and what happens. In *A Different Set of Stars*, twin girls go to Brazil. First, they pack. Next, they arrive at the lodge. Then they cannot find the Big Dipper at night. Last, they learn why the stars look different south of the equator.

Your Turn

Imagine you are writing a fiction story about what people see in the daytime or nighttime sky. Make a sequence chart that shows First, Next, Then, and Last. Write one thing that happens in each part of the story.